Creature Features

Creature Tails

nicola whittaker

KU-622-979

First published in 2001 by
Franklin Watts
96 Leonard Street
London
WC2A 4XD

© Franklin Watts 2001

Franklin Watts Australia
56 O'Riordan Street
Alexandria
NSW 2015

Editor: Samantha Armstrong
Designer: Jason Anscomb
Science consultant: Dr Jim Flegg

ISBN: 0 7496 4026 X
Dewey Decimal Number: 591.1
A CIP number for this book is available from the British Library

DUDLEY PUBLIC LIBRARIES

L   45343

153683   SCH

J 591.4

Picture credits:
NHPA: Cover: James Carmichael Jr; Yves Lanceau; Stephen
Dalton; 5 Martin Harvey; 6-7 A.N.T.; 8-9 Henry Ausloos;
10 Manfred Danegger; 11 Stephen Dalton; 12-13 Kevin Schafer;
16 Andy Rouse; 17 T. Kitchin and V. Hurst; 18-19 Yves Lanceau;
19 Anthony Bannister; 20-21 Daniel Heuclin; 22-23 Daniel
Heuclin; 25 Nigel J. Dennis.
Oxford Scientific Films: 4 J. and P. Wegner.
Planet Earth Pictures: 14-15 Geoff Du Feu; 24 Steve Bloom.
Franklin Watts Photo Library: 26-27.
Printed in Hong Kong/China

Creature Features

Creature Tails

nicola whittaker

W

FRANKLIN WATTS
LONDON·SYDNEY

Different creatures have

4

different tails.

5

Some have scales,

6

some have hair.

Some tails are bushy,

others are bare.

some tails are **short,**

13

some tails are long.

This tail is curly,

this tail can pong!

17

Some tails like to wag...

18

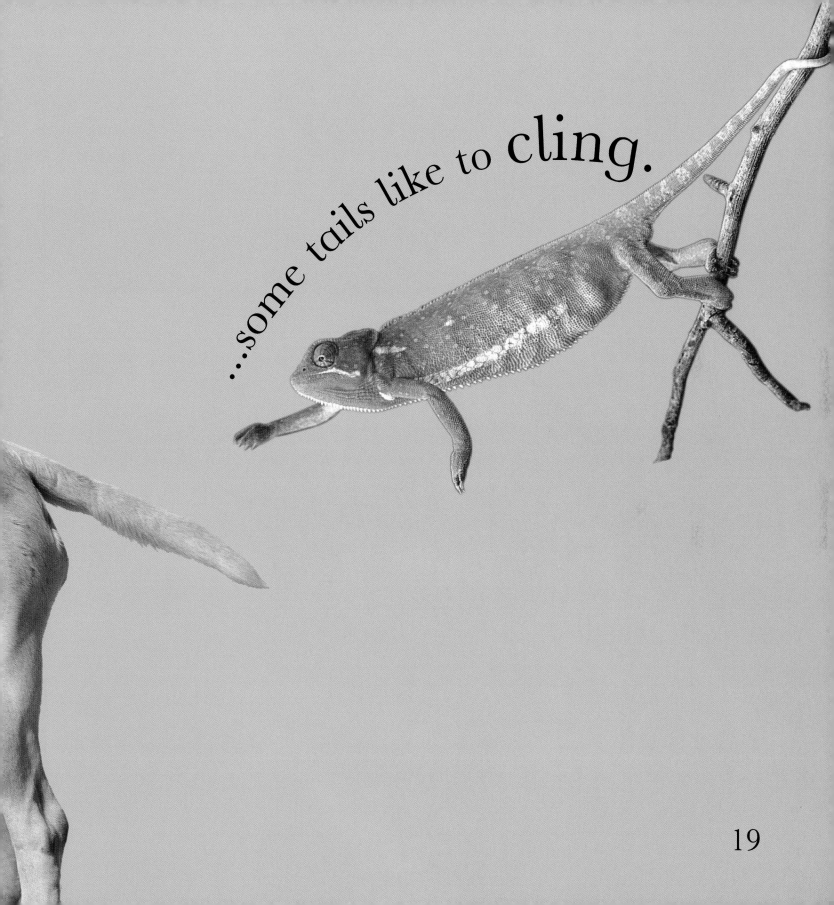

...some tails like to cling.

19

Some tails can *rattle,*

others can

sting!

Some tails like to swim.

Some tails have eyes...

but my
tail is

missing...

Can you tell me

why?

Glossary

Budgerigar
(Melopsittacus undulatus)
Bird (parrot family)
Lives: Central Australia
Eats: Seeds
Lives in huge flocks in the
wild.

Ring-Tailed Lemur
(Lemur catta)
Mammal (primate family)
Lives: Madagascar
Eats: Leaves
Uses its long tail to signal to
others in its group.

Siamese Fighting Fish
(Betta splendens)
Fish (freshwater teleost family)
Lives: Rivers in South East Asia
Eats: Small animals
Often kept in aquariums, but
now rarely found in the wild.

White Horses
(Equus caballus)
Mammal (horse family)
Lives: Worldwide
Eats: Grass
The horse's prehistoric ancestors
originated in America.

Red Squirrel
(Sciurus vulgaris)
Mammal (rat family)
Lives: European forests
Eats: Nuts and berries
Uses its tail to shelter from cold winds and rain.

Black Rat
(Rattus rattus)
Mammal (rat family)
Lives: Now rare, but once worldwide
Eats: Almost anything
Famous for spreading the deadly Plague to many countries.

Bob Cat
(Felis rufus)
Mammal (cat family)
Lives: North America
Eats: Small mammals and birds
Usually hunts after dark.

Emperor Dragonfly
(Anax imperator)
Insect (dragonfly family)
Lives: Widespread
Eats: Insects
Unlike other insects, dragon-flies cannot fold their wings.

Glossary

Pig
(Sus scrofa)
Mammal (pig family)
Lives: Farms worldwide
Eats: Anything
Grubs up food with its
powerful nose.

Striped Skunk
(Mephitis mephitis)
Mammal (weasel and badger family)
Lives: North America
Eats: Mice and insects
Squirts smelly liquid when
attacked.

Dog
(Canis familiaris)
Mammal (dog family)
Lives: Worldwide
Eats: Most things
Originally descended from
wolves.

Chameleon
(Chameleo dilepis)
Reptile (lizard family)
Lives: South Africa
Eats: Insects
Can hold on to twigs with its
curly tail.

Rattlesnake
(Crotalis sp.)
Reptile (snake family)
Lives: North American deserts
Eats: Small animals, e.g. mice
Rattles the tip of its tail to
warn off enemies.

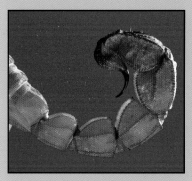

Fat-tailed Scorpion
(Androctonus australis)
Arachnia (spider family)
Lives: Australian deserts
Eats: Insects
Defends itself and kills prey
with its poisonous sting.

Bottlenose Dolphins
(Tursiops truncatus)
Mammal (whale/porpoise family)
Lives: North Atlantic Ocean
Eats: Fish and squids
Its powerful tail fins are
actually its back legs and feet.

Peacock
(Pavo cristatus)
Bird (pheasant family)
Lives: Asia
Eats: Plants, seeds and snails
The male displays its gorgeous
tail to attract females.

Index

Entries in italics refer to pictures.